301.43
KEE

77-454

MILTON HENRY KEENE

Abingdon • Nashville

EPWORTH METHODIST CHURCH
HOPE VALLEY ROAD
DURHAM, NORTH CAROLINA

Patterns for Mature Living

Copyright © 1976 by Abingdon

All rights reserved.
No part of this book may be reproduced in any manner whatsoever without written permission of the publisher except brief quotations embodied in critical articles or reviews. For information address Abingdon, Nashville, Tennessee.

Library of Congress Catalog Card Number: 76-27093

ISBN 0-687-30385-0

Scripture quotations unless otherwise noted are from the Revised Standard Version of the Bible, copyrighted 1946, 1952, © 1971, 1973 by the Division of Christian Education, National Council of Churches, and are used by permission.

MANUFACTURED BY THE PARTHENON PRESS AT
NASHVILLE, TENNESSEE, UNITED STATES OF AMERICA

To Dot
—my wife and dearest friend

CONTENTS

PART ONE
You Are Not Your Age 9

  1. You Are Not Your Age 11
  2. You're As Young As Ever—and As Old 13
  3. Make the Best of the Rest
     of Your Days 15
  4. Better Than a Mirror 17

PART TWO
Coming to Terms with Life 19

  5. The Unknown Glory of Life 21
  6. Eighteen Square Feet of Reality 23
  7. Your Place in the Universe 25
  8. Where Do You Live? 27
  9. Your Greatest Freedom 29
 10. Keep Your Life Flowing 31
 11. You're Stronger Than You Think 33
 12. Be Patient with Yourself 35
 13. Believe What You Can 37
 14. Alone—with Yourself 39
 15. Making a Comeback 41
 16. Turning Misfortune into
     Good Fortune 43
 17. Don't Say Impossible! 45
 18. Find the Right Handle 47
 19. Extend Your Life's Boundaries 49
 20. Keep Your Life Adjusted 51
 21. How to Rout the Hounds of Fear 53
 22. How to "Case" Your Fears 55
 23. Stuck in a Corner? 57

24. How to Make Life Less Boring 59
25. Don't Let a Problem Blot
    Out the World 61
26. Loneliness—Causes and Cures 63
27. Shatter Lonely Silence with a Song 65
28. Moving Toward Love 67
29. When You Feel Like an Ant,
    Act Like One 69
30. Life Does Not Have to Be Drab 71
31. Use Your Five Senses 73
32. Plant a Garden 75
33. To Know One Good Old Man 77
34. One Good Old Man 79
35. Your Life's Prevailing Winds 81
36. Your Invincible Surmise 83
37. Recapturing Life's Lost Chord 85
38. A Certain Grace 87

PART THREE
The Souls of All Seasons 89

39. The Beautiful People 91
40. The Best Thing You Have 93
41. Be a Good Listener 95
42. Priming the Old Pump 97
43. Hate: the Mask of Fear 99
44. At Peace with the World 101
45. Keep Your Lights Burning 103
46. The Hurt and the Healing of People .. 105

PART FOUR
The Ultimate Relationship 107

47. A Higher Point of View 109
48. Without Majority Vote 111

PART ONE
You Are Not Your Age

1. You Are Not Your Age

"I am who I am." —Exodus 3:13

You are not your age, and your age is not you. This is so obvious when viewed logically that it would seem unnecessary to point it out—except that even the most logical-minded people are sometimes not too logical when they begin to think about their age.

The two-digit figure which you write solemnly on legal forms, applications for automobile operator's license renewal, and the like, is just one more statistical fact about you—like your height, weight, and shoe size.

Of course, it is a very personal fact, and it does say something about you; but it certainly doesn't begin to say everything about you—and probably none of the really important things.

The French, as I recall from my brief exposure to their language, have another, and I think better, way of referring to age than we have. It may amount to the same thing in the long run, but when a Frenchman says, "I have sixty years," it just occurs to me that there's more living and breathing space between him and his age than there is for the American who says, "I'm sixty years old."

The French way of saying it makes a person's age one of his many possessions—along with his house, his car, his wardrobe, and his pet dog.

It's this feeling of liberating distance, uncramped and uncrowded space, between the person and his age, which carries with it the sense of freedom that makes him know that he is whatever he is, whatever his age.

It may well be that one important reason why some persons—young and old alike—are reluctant to reveal their age is simply that they are unwilling to let an impersonal figure stand for all that they are, whether in their own esteem or in the thinking of others.

The teen-ager who is fifteen may not want to be thought of as just fifteen, because he is a person with ideas, convictions, abilities, and feelings that he does not want to have obscured by the empty and impersonal significance of a number. With the sensitivity of the young—which is not too different from that of the aging—he is aware that he can be summarily dismissed as "only fifteen" from any serious family or community discussion, and he does not want to risk this.

The seventy-five-year-old man feels the same way. If he can be counted out of life because he's a certain age, who can blame him for being none too willing to say how old he is?

The great apostle whose name was Paul wrote to his young friend Timothy, "Let no man despise thy youth." He was in effect saying, "Don't let anyone judge you by your age only and thus discount you as an individual with rich personal resources."

2. You're As Young As Ever —and As Old

"Like a householder who brings out of his treasure what is new and what is old." —Matthew 13:52

Like a tree, a human life carries within itself every age of its life—from one to seventy and beyond. Some place within you, you are still six years old. Locked away in one of those annual rings of your life, there are all of the bright, fresh impressions of your sixth summer.

If you dare, if you're not afraid of seeming "foolish," you can reach back and feel it all again anytime you choose: bare feet walking through grass dripping with the dew of a summer morning; gliding through the snow of a bright December day on a sled drawn by your father; kicking through the red and gold leaves of an autumn day; gathering acorns beneath the spreading branches of a prolific oak tree. It's all there—that freshness and sense of wonder. The only reason it seems so remote is that you have pushed it all out of your maturing life—as though it no longer had any value for you.

All of those throbbing hopes and poignant feelings of your seventeenth year are still with you. Yes, someplace within you, you are still seventeen, and the birds are singing and the skies are bright. There, the waves of an expanding appreciation of life are still washing the shore.

Among the most interesting people in the world are persons past sixty. They have assimilated the flavor of all their years, and they are at peace with themselves. They no longer strive for maturity; they possess it in every ripened, full-flavored insight of their mature minds. They're old enough not to be ashamed of having been young once, and in their present years they revel still in the radiant pools of the past.

Observe a man in his sixties or seventies sitting beside a stream with a five-year-old boy, his grandson or a neighbor's child. Watch them closely and you will be aware of a comradeship as intimate as if they were the same age. The fact is, they are. The man is mature enough to permit himself to reach back to the fifth annual ring of his own life, and so he feels what the little five-year-old feels—seeing, touching, wondering at the quiet ripples of the passing current as when he was a boy.

It isn't enough to have been twelve once and only once—to have been nineteen only one time. Human life is something like cutting a record—you go through the experience at the moment in order that it might be yours as long as you live, yours as often as you place the disk on the turntable and set the needle in the groove.

The fact is—if you're willing to have it so—you are as young as you've ever been, and as old. If you will accept this, and range freely through the sunlight and shade of your own life, your present life will assume new, wonderful dimensions—new colors, sounds, sensations. Yet they won't really be new, since you have known them, loved them, thrilled to them all before.

3. Make the Best of the Rest of Your Days

"Awake, and strengthen what remains."
—Revelation 3:2

A man I know says that if he had his life to live over, he'd travel more. Another person vows he would get a better education. Another says he would make more friends. A woman in her seventies declares she would write a book.

This all sounds good. But unless a person is doing something in line right then with what he says he would do if he could live his life over, he probably wouldn't do it if he had three more lifetimes.

A person doesn't have to live his life over to do some of the things he says he'd do if he had that chance.

Who ever said you had to live your life over to get a better education? Some of the best-educated persons in the world are men and women who have educated themselves—many of them in the second half of their lives. Furthermore, colleges and high schools throughout America are offering courses to older people who want to improve their minds. Television offers educational opportunities to people who turn their TV dials to the right channel. Some retirement residences offer educational courses to their residents and to other older persons in the community.

Who ever said you had to live your life over to make more friends? I have observed some of the closest friendships develop between people in their seventies and beyond. "We found each other!" an older woman told me recently when I commented on her lovely friendship with another woman who lives in the same

15

retirement community. Their friendship is the joy of their lives—and they didn't know each other until a little over two years ago.

You can never get back the first of your days, but you can make some of the most cherished friendships of your life in the rest of your days if you make the effort.

And who ever said you have to live your life over to be helpful to the human race? I know a lady in her eighties whose great joy it is to fold bandages for the local hospital. She smiles with pride when she has folded ten thousand of them.

Instead of letting yourself sentimentalize about what you would do if you had the impossible chance to live your life over, why not give some thought to what you can do with the rest of your life.

The chances are you've got far more to work with in terms of human understanding, emotional maturity, and genuine ability than you ever had earlier in your life.

Plan to make the most of the rest of your days—and maybe, like Job, you can make the rest the best.

4. Better Than a Mirror

Now we see in a mirror dimly, but then face to face. —I Corinthians 13:12

In Leo Tolstoy's *Death of Ivan Ilych,* there is a description that anyone on the western slope of life's craggy mountain can appreciate:

> Ivan Ilych began to wash. With pauses for rest, he washed his hands and then his face, cleaned his teeth, brushed his hair, and looked in the glass. He was terrified by what he saw, especially the limp way in which his hair clung to his pallid forehead. While his shirt was being changed he knew that he would be still more frightened at the sight of his body, so he avoided looking at it.

If the mirror test ever was of any value in enabling an individual to arrive at a reasonable self-evaluation, by the time he reaches sixty, he might consider a substitute method.

As life moves past its meridian, there might well be a deliberate reduction in the number of times one looks into the looking glass. Were you ever lastingly reassured by what looked back at you from the mirror?

When you were twelve or twenty, thirty or forty—did you ever honestly feel that you were in touch with the most vital version of yourself in the mirror image?

Persons past fifty or sixty need to explore other methods of self-perception.

Suggestion? Yes, here's one—talk.

Out of the unmeasured depths of your deepest thoughts and convictions, your most sincere beliefs, aspirations, hopes and dreams, talk to another human being. Or perhaps better still under some circumstances, write it down.

Then listen to what you're saying, or read it back. Hear yourself pouring forth with the priceless treasures of your soul. That's you speaking—you, the real person—not a mirror impression. The deeply earnest voice, the bit of humor coming through completely unrehearsed—that is you—deeply, honestly, truly you. Does it sound young, happy, adventurous at times; at times bold and carefree? That's you!

While writing *Treasure Island,* Robert Louis Stevenson was a sick man—a bag of bones according to the mirror version of himself. But writing from the unfathomable depths of his being, he experienced himself in what you might call an eternal dimension that neither age, ill health, misfortune, nor anything else that can happen to mortal man could change in the slightest.

Keep in touch with the eternity that dwells within you if you want to keep in touch with your truest self. It's far more telling than a mirror.

PART TWO
Coming to Terms with Life

5. The Unknown Glory of Life

"Blessed are the eyes which see what you see!"
—Luke 10:23

I walked into a picture on a recent autumn evening—stepped right through the frame and stood there in silence, seeing, feeling, breathing the unspeakable glory of the scene.

It was late in October, and the full moon was spilling its silver into the dark waters of the river. A brisk wind brushed the surface, breaking it up into millions of liquid facets mirroring the moonlight.

When I first saw it, the moon was barely above the eastern rim of the world, shimmering through a leafy filigree of trees that lined the river shore.

The bridge crossing the river was a narrow black ribbon dividing the broad silvery path. Along the highway moved an occasional car or truck whose headlights added a touch of gold to the silvery wonder of the scene.

Drawn by the full moon, I had slipped out of the house and stood on the river bank. In the foreground were two large trees, a sweet gum and a hackberry, both of whose leaves a week ago had been scarlet; now they were entering their russet phase.

The rough bark of the tall trees framed the quiet moonlight vista. Stepping past them I felt that I had become part of the picture. It was no longer an object of which I was the beholder. I was now part of it and it, part of me.

Those cars gliding along the silhouette of the bridge were part of it too. But did their occupants know it? Or did they pass without knowing?

Were they so concerned with where they were going that they failed to realize where they were? Were they so caught up in anticipation of other hours and other places that they missed the glory of this time and this place? Had the ugly brush strokes of the cares of this world vandalized for them this exquisite canvas revealing the glory of this world?

Could this be the fate of mankind—to be part of a vast and lovely picture and never know it, to never suspect the glory that embraces life?

Must it always be this way? Can't someone who sees it tell it? If there had been a public address system at hand that would have enabled me to reach the ears of those in the passing cars and trucks, I would have announced to them: "May I have your attention, please... You are passing through a lovely moonscape, and you are part of it."

Come to think of it, this is the kind of thing that Jesus of Nazareth did in the days of his flesh. He told men and women that they were part of an everlasting glory. Their nights and days were embraced by it, their hours and moments immersed in it.

Some believed him, and for them, life took on glorious new meaning. They became new creatures for whom old things had passed away, and behold, all things had become new.

6. Eighteen Square Feet of Reality

"Ask the beasts, and they will teach you; the birds of the air, and they will tell you." —Job 12:7

Slouching lazily on the front porch of the aging frame house located at the edge of the little country town, I found myself involved in a kind of game.

Since every game must have its rules and boundaries, I decreed that the limits of my game would be the main panel of the screened-in porch with its well-defined borders of pine framing.

The game would be this: I would note and observe each of the varied aspects of rural life that I could see within this limited field of vision. I would require myself to identify it, describe it, make some comment on its history, background, or habits.

Most obvious among the objects before my eyes were the trunks of three giant poplar trees. Often had I gazed at them and whimsically imagined them to be the legs of some giant creature of a bygone day.

Now I studied them. What did I really know about these trees? What could I tell someone else about them? In what respects were they different from other trees—like the Norway maples shading the lawn directly in front of where I was sitting? What if any historic events had occurred beneath trees like these?

Frankly, I was obliged to confess, I just plain did not know. Of course, I could have come up with some comment on items made out of poplar wood—like Dutch shoes; but I'm not even sure I knew that then!

As I continued to gaze out through the screen panel, a beautiful red bird dropped down near one of the giant trees, attracted by a bread crumb. It was a

23

cardinal, with its red, crested head bobbing eagerly as it pecked at the small white lump.

Again I asked myself what I knew about these lovely birds that delight the eye as they wing through the blue of the sky or perch in the shimmering green of an English holly tree. Though they have thrilled me since boyhood, I was forced to admit to myself I knew precious little about them.

Then came the butterflies in frail, nervous flight through the summer morning breeze. Again, a question. And, once more, pitifully inadequate answers.

My game wasn't doing at all well; and yet perhaps it was. At least it was reminding me that there's more to be seen through eighteen square feet of porch screen than many a man and woman can appreciate in a lifetime.

It also reminded me that if my life should ever become limited to what I could see, hear, smell, and touch in a pitifully small area of this wide world, there would be enough in it to keep me wondering in amazement the rest of my life.

7. Your Place in the Universe

"What is man that thou art mindful of him?"
—Hebrews 2:6

For anyone who has forgotten (or never known) his intimate relationship with heaven and earth, a reading of Alexis Carrel's book *Reflections on Life* is stimulating and immensely reassuring.

Far from being independent or of a different order of reality, a human being is part and parcel of the earth he walks on, the air he breathes, and the heaven to which he lifts his wondering eyes.

The greater part of the human body is the water that descends in summer rains and then bubbles up in springs that become streams and rivers flowing to the sea.

The next time you look out your window at the silver of falling rain and frown because it's going to dampen your clothes a little or undo your hairdo, remember—if the water of past rainfalls had not filtered into every cell of your body, you wouldn't even be here to see the rain falling gently against your window.

Do not deal with rain as though it were an enemy. It is your life. And the more sensitive you are to the intimacy of the relationship, the more you will appreciate your human existence and your place in this vast scheme of an unspeakable creation.

The chemical components of our bodies are the same as those which form sun, moon, and stars. Carrel reminds us that the hydrogen in a molecule of glycogen found in the liver and muscle fibers of a human being as well as the calcium that forms human bones are the same hydrogen and calcium contained in the flaming furnace of the sun.

Think about this the next time you see the sun burning through the mists of an autumn morning just as the birds begin to waken and the earth to bathe itself in amber light. The sun is no alien creation. The elements in its prodigious flames stoke the fires of life within you.

When a meteorite penetrates Earth's atmosphere in a flaming dive, it carries with it the same kind of iron that flows in your bloodstream.

Floating in interstellar space are sodium atoms no different than the salt in your saltshaker which could be used to season your breakfast eggs tomorrow morning.

You are a part of the universe; and there is a sense in which the universe accepts and respects its own when its own comes to it not as a stranger.

Our tragic human error is that we are inclined to set ourselves against the natural world that sustains us. We come to it as plunderers, pillagers, saboteurs, and exploiters. When we are not raping it, we assume a contemptuous indifference toward it, as though we were somehow above the mighty forces which shape rocks and stars and trees.

The laws of the Creator of all things in heaven and earth are written into our bodies and brains. When we affirm and honor them, we affirm and honor ourselves.

8. Where Do You Live?

Keep your heart with all vigilance; for from it flow the springs of life. —Proverbs 4:23

"I would not choose to be living in any other place or at any other time," said an aging Englishwoman whose house had just been bombed during one of the London air raids.

Such a spirit is stimulating and refreshing in a day when many people wish they had been born a hundred years earlier or later, or that they might have emerged in Australia or Africa instead of America, or that they might have missed the painful experience of life altogether.

How could the Englishwoman have said such a thing under the circumstances? The answer had more to do with her inner life than any of its external conditions. Where she lived, how she lived were matters of the spirit, not of mere time and geography.

Where do you live? Whether you have established residence in London, Washington, Philadelphia, or some other place, your real address is a state of mind.

There will always be people who will feel that if they could just move away from where they're living, everything would be all right.

But in most cases, moving from one location to another would make little if any difference, for the simple reason that a human being, like a turtle, carries his place of abode with him wherever he goes. "The mind is its own place, and in itself can make a heaven of hell, a hell of heaven," wrote the poet Milton in *Paradise Lost*.

I always enjoy watching people working on their

houses—painting, building new dormer windows, landscaping the garden. But one can't help wondering what kind of improvements they're making in the place they will live for the rest of their lives—their own minds.

If things are orderly there, if thought blends harmoniously with thought, and feeling accords with feeling, then life is always livable, and a person can be daily glad he's alive.

Like the Englishwoman during the London air raids, a person can be in the midst of war and still experience a deep inner peace. But in the midst of peace and plenty, an individual who has never made peace with his own soul and his God is like a beleaguered city about to crumble.

Paul, the apostle of Jesus who lived his life with intensity, wrote a letter once in which he said, "I have learned in whatsoever state I am therewith to be content."

He could say that and mean it because it didn't matter to him where he was physically—whether in a Greek port city, in a mountain hut in Turkey, in a Roman jail, or shipwrecked in the Mediterranean—his true state was the state of his mind, a mind made whole through faith in Christ.

9. Your Greatest Freedom

We rejoice in our sufferings, knowing that suffering produces endurance, and endurance produces character, and character produces hope. —Romans 5:3-4

One of the greatest challenges of life beyond sixty is coping with an eroding freedom, fought for over a lifetime, won at high cost.

The right to drive a car (one of the "hooray" experiences of growing up), the freedom to stay up until twelve o'clock, the liberty to go and come as one pleases—all of these hard-won privileges come under attack in the years beyond sixty.

"I've had to give up driving; I can't get around like I once did; I'm beginning to wonder if I'm going to have any freedom left in another ten years," said a man in his seventies.

The basic freedom of a human being is something he can sustain until his last breath. No outside force can take it from him. No sickness or accident can erode it.

When a person realizes he possesses such freedom, he feels himself being lifted above chance and circumstance. It makes him a winner in the conflict of life.

Viktor Frankl, a Viennese physician, in his book *The Doctor and the Soul* observed of his fellow prisoners in Auschwitz, the notorious concentration camp where he spent the years of the Second World War, that whatever may have been taken from them in their first hour in camp, "until his last breath no one can wrest from a man his freedom to take one or another attitude toward his destiny."

The freedom to select the attitude that you will have

toward whatever happens to you in this world—this is undoubtedly mankind's greatest freedom.

Many a person has a secret list of things he knows he could never bear. One of these may be loss of sight. "I know I just couldn't live if I should ever go blind," somebody says.

A young American, a soldier wounded in action, visited every significant and lovely spot in Europe before he returned to the States. "I'm going blind," he said, "so I'm painting pictures on the canvas of my mind."

No doubt this young man had once thought that he could never bear blindness, but with this attitude, he knew he could handle it.

Ralph Erskine, racked with pain, said, "I have known more of God since I came to this bed than through all my life." So, for this man, sickness, through his choice of attitude, became a supreme opportunity to become better acquainted with God.

Always, no matter what happens to you or what may be taken from you, there will remain the greatest freedom—to choose the attitude with which you will deal with your life.

It was a man who well knew this ultimate freedom, who survived imprisonment, shipwreck, and stoning that nearly killed him, who said, "We are more than conquerors through him who loved us" (Rom. 8:37).

10. Keep Your Life Flowing

Like streams of water in a dry place . . .
—Isaiah 32:2

"My life is like the Brandywine—in some places clear and calm, in other places swift, churning and muddy." This was the way a friend of mine characterized his existence.

There's a freshness about the figure of speech, and an insight worth considering. Take a stroll beside the Brandywine on a crisp fall morning, or along the banks of any other creek or stream that has character, and the analogy of the flow of the stream to the flow of life is irresistible.

There are, for example, quiet places, where the current is lazy and restful to the eye of the observer and the calm surface mirrors the shapes of tall oaks and sycamores and, above them, the blue of a cloudless sky. Life is like that at times.

Farther downstream the placid water feels the tug of a swifter current, and the stream goes tumbling over mossy rocks that churn the water into white foam. There are times when the boulders in the creek bed seem almost impassable; but the current finds a way through, and so the creek flows on toward the river, and beyond that the bay, and then the ocean.

The all-important characteristic of a stream is its flowing quality. Lovely it need not be, nor picturesque, nor fascinating. But flow it must if it is a stream making its way to the sea. Even in its quiet places, cool with the shade of giant trees, where movement is nearly imperceptible, a leaf or a twig floating on the surface soon disappears from sight, carried along by the stream's flow.

Perhaps it is here that the Brandywine, or any other creek, bears its finest analogy to human life. Life, whatever happens to it, must continue to flow until it reaches its destination. Through rocks that tear at it, over dams that temporarily block its course, twisting, turning, swirling, eddying—it must go on.

In life, as in a creek, the treacherous places are not where the water dashes around and against obstacles in foaming eagerness, but where the current is breached by a dam. There the natural flow is impeded.

The dammed-up waters of human thought and feeling are sullen, bitter, dangerous waters. There the currents turn back upon themselves, creating whirlpools that suck whatever is on the surface down to murky depths.

Keep your life flowing, through rocks, past narrows that seem to threaten its passage, down steep declivities. Keep it flowing.

Life, like the Brandywine, that lovely creek of my boyhood rambles, was meant to flow, to move out from its springs, and to be fulfilled at last in the great seas of God.

11. You're Stronger Than You Think

Let thy hand be upon . . . the son of man whom thou hast made strong. —Psalm 80:17

You're stronger than you think you are. Many people have frail, shrinking-violet notions about themselves, when the truth of the matter is, they're more like oaks.

How can we bring our notions about ourselves into closer harmony with the facts? The answer lies in a rocky, forbidding region of human experience which many of us avoid as long as we can—suffering. Nobody, however, can ever completely avoid it. In one form or another, it comes to all. Hence, every day men and women emerge from harrowing encounters, grueling contests with suffering, worn but with new light in their eyes—the light of personal discovery.

When a woman learned that her house was on fire, she ran the entire five-mile distance home. Discussing the event some weeks afterward, she said excitedly, "I didn't know I could do it!"

It is through occasional bouts with trouble in one of its many forms that we discover within ourselves what might be called our endurance factor.

After a month without sleeping, a man who thought that a half-dozen sleepless nights would certainly do him in, stands straight and strong, pulse even, his mind still capable of thinking clearly. He's amazed to find himself not only still alive, but functioning normally.

He just didn't know he had it in him. But now he knows he has—and the knowledge will serve him well the rest of his days. He knows he's made of tougher stuff, with more built-in endurance than he had ever dreamed.

Many people unfit themselves for the rigors of life by imagining that they're weak when actually they're strong.

Those who climb the forbidding heights of Mount Everest are men in quest of something within themselves—and they're begging the mountain to help them find it. What it is, is the capacity to endure and continue to function, which most of us possess but nevertheless remain unacquainted with until some kind of extreme physical or mental demand reveals it.

What is it in a human being that enables him to hold on and keep going when it seems the last fiber of muscle and body cell seem exhausted? These "Everesters" want to know—and in the last agonizing inches between them and the great white summit, they find it.

Regardless of your age, physical condition, or any other circumstance, you can figure that by and large you're a whole lot stronger than you think, and you can take much more than some of your shrinking-violet notions of yourself would lead you to believe. God made you that way. Learn to trust what he has made!

12. Be Patient with Yourself

"In your patience ye shall win your souls."
—Luke 21:19

The man in the bowling alley with his team was getting disgusted with himself. Twice he had guttered the ball. Then he missed three straight spares. His game was ruined.

Turning away from the gleaming maple wood of the alley he wagged his head, slumped in his seat, and muttered words of self-reproach.

He was the unhappiest man in the place. His face was a frowning flag of self-defeat. A teammate, aware of his friend's feelings, slipped down next to him and through the thunder of falling tenpins, whispered, "Take it easy, Joe. Have some patience with yourself!"

Joe smiled and indicated that he'd try.

Next time up Joe made his spare and came back to his seat feeling somewhat better. His game improved progressively after that.

Getting back into his street shoes after the game, he winked at his teammate gratefully. "Thanks for the tip," he said.

It's a tip that many people need. Have patience with yourself!

Most people would be too considerate to show toward others the degree of impatience that they regularly inflict upon themselves.

Consider some of the impatient comments you address to yourself in those inner conversations that we all conduct from time to time.

You mislaid your door key, and you have to ask somebody to help you get in. You're embarrassed over the situation and angry with yourself. Sternly you tell yourself that such a thing should never happen; people should remember their door keys.

Now if you were on the other side of this situation, and instead of being the one needing help, you were the one giving it, you would show all kinds of patience with the other person.

"Don't feel bad about that," you might say, "it happens to us all from time to time."

Why can't we be as patient with ourselves as with others? It may be because we expect more of ourselves. It's as if we set ourselves apart as being somewhat superior, and when something happens to remind us that we're not, it frustrates us.

There comes a time in every individual's life when he must recognize that he has the same proneness to mistakes as everybody else; that in all probability he is not a glowing, outstanding exception to nature's rule, but truly one of nature's average people; and that just as other people can make mistakes, so can he.

When an individual recognizes and accepts this fact, he will become a more patient person—toward others and himself.

Without becoming self-indulgent, many people could help themselves considerably by having a little bit of patience with themselves when the going gets difficult.

13. Believe What You Can

"I believe; help my unbelief!"   —Mark 9:24

"My doubts bother me," wrote a man who said he's middle-aged. "I've been brought up in the church, and I've repeated the creeds Sunday after Sunday. I believe them while I'm still in church; but when I leave, they leave. What can I do about my doubts?"

Somebody could suggest that he stay in church all the time, but that would be impossible, and even undesirable.

Faith that needs the props of liturgy, organ music, preaching, and congregational singing to support it is not the kind of faith that will sustain a human being in some harrowing hour out there in the world when the voices of worship are silent and the din of the market place is in his ears.

There is one thing he should not do about his doubts, and that is deny he has them. If he does that, he'll be untrue to himself. A dependable faith can't rest on such a foundation.

The best thing to do with an honest doubt is to face it. Admit to yourself you have it, though you don't want it. Then turn to the one or two things you honestly believe, and begin to live like you believe them.

This may leave you with a very small bundle of faith, but don't worry about the size of the package so long as what's in it is real to you. Jesus once said that if a person has faith as small as a grain of mustard seed, he can move a mountain!

A friend told me that after he had faced all his honest doubts there was only one thing left that he really believed without reservation. That one thing was love. He believed that it is the greatest thing in the world.

Putting aside all the things he didn't believe, he turned to this one thing he believed with all his heart and mind. Slowly, thoughtfully, he began to build his life around this spark that glowed amid the ashes.

Gradually he committed bits of his daily living to the spark, like shreds of bark from a dry tree. The spark became a flame, and the flame became a warm, friendly fire glowing in the chill night.

Then, like children coming in from the cold, drawn by the cheerful camp fire, many of the things that he had put aside because he had doubts about them moved into the friendly light of what the man truly believed.

As time went on, most of the things he once doubted were standing in the circle of his truest faith. There were still a few doubts here and there, and he faced them honestly. But in the glow of the faith that was his by day and night, in storms and beneath clear skies, all that he had ever believed returned to him.

14. Alone—with Yourself

Be strengthened ... through his Spirit in the inner man. —Ephesians 3:16

The judge stepped into the little four-by-four elevator in the Federal Courthouse in New York City just as he had done hundreds of times before; but this time the elevator stalled, and the judge was trapped for forty minutes, alone.

Afterward, someone asked him how he felt.

"Have you ever been alone with yourself in a stalled elevator?" the judge asked. Then he explained that it wasn't the forty minutes lost out of a busy schedule that bothered him, nor was it that he feared the elevator wouldn't be repaired and himself "rescued." It was the fact that he was alone with himself for forty minutes, without the usual ego supports which come from the presence of other human beings.

"I just made a horrible discovery," he said, stepping from the elevator, "I'm the dullest company in the world."

What had happened in those forty minutes in the judge's mind? We can only guess from his words.

One thought might have been that after all these years in the public eye, in the private eye of his own self-awareness, he really didn't know himself. Locked in the stalled elevator alone, he was not a judge, a well-known figure, but just a human being.

Maybe once at least in those lonely minutes, the thought crossed his mind that if this four-by-four cubicle that contained him were turned over to horizontal position, it wouldn't seem unlike a casket.

One of the best things any person can do for himself

is to make his own acquaintance so that when he's alone, he's not with a stranger but a good friend whom he knows and likes.

A human being becomes a stranger to himself the moment he accepts the ideas and feelings of other people as his own instead of holding to his own.

This happens early, when we are too young and innocent to defend ourselves against the conspiracy which, before it is finished, alienates us from our truest, most honest thoughts and feelings.

To regain the lost Eden of our own pure, uncompromised soul, we must re-educate ourselves to know what we truly think, feel, believe, want, like, and dislike.

It may turn out that others reject the way we feel about life and reject us for feeling the way we do. But then, the big question is: are we willing to become strangers to ourselves in order that we might seem to be friends to strangers? No one wins this way in the end—especially the person who feels at home only with others and a stranger to himself when he's alone.

There's still something to be said for those words that begin, "To thine own self be true . . ."

15. Making a Comeback

Lift your drooping hands and strengthen your weak knees, . . . so that what is lame may . . . be healed.
—Hebrews 12:12-13

It was not the usual game of checkers that the two men were playing. In the first place, the board was hanging from the wall.

The black and red squares each had a wooden dowel stuck into it. The checkers, about three inches in diameter, had holes drilled through their middles, doughnutlike, so that they could be hung on the dowels.

Between the players, standing close to the wall, there was the same happy banter which usually surrounds a checker board.

At first glance everything else appeared quite normal.

The occupational therapist leaned close and whispered to me confidentially that these two men were victims of CVA—cerebral vascular accident, or stroke. It had partially paralyzed them; now they were attempting to make a comeback.

"You're cheating!" the therapist chided. The cheating was not of the usual variety for checkers. It was the fact that the man had used his good hand to reach up and grasp the checker. There followed a ripple of laughter, and the next move he made was fair—in the sense that he used the hand on his bad side to execute it.

It would have been much easier for each man to use the part of his body unaffected by the CVA, but this would not have helped him to make his comeback.

He could have played a better game of checkers, but the game was secondary to the main objective of regaining use of the affected member. And the only way to do that was to have the courage to be awkward.

The game as they were playing it was an exercise in three simple manual processes that most people take for granted—reach, grasp, and release. For these men these simple processes had become painfully difficult.

Only after I fully understood the handicap involved was I able to appreciate the courage of these two checker players.

Yes, it would have been easier for them to use their stronger hands. And easier than this would have been not to play the game at all, or not to accept physical therapy. Easiest of all would have been just to sit back and be waited on the rest of their lives.

The road back is never easy, but the company you meet as you travel it are brave souls who ask nothing more than a chance to make the next move. And the sense of triumph of spirit over flesh that comes when like a salmon swimming upstream, leaping the rapids, running the falls, you find yourself in still waters at last, with only the memory of the herculean effort behind you and the surge of new life within you, makes you know it was worth those days and nights of grim discipline. Then, you are not just one more human being shaped by forces beyond your command; you are a conqueror.

16. Turning Misfortune into Good Fortune

"You meant evil . . . but God meant . . . good."
—Genesis 50:20

In the town of Enterprise, Alabama, there's a monument that honors the source of a southern tragedy—the Mexican boll weevil.

When the cotton-consuming beetle first appeared in Coffee County in the year 1915, the annual cotton yield of thirty-five thousand bales was cut forty percent.

Gradually, the weevil devastated the entire cotton belt—from Texas to Georgia. With bankruptcy facing them, the cotton farmers were forced to turn to diversified farming.

That's when they began to grow corn, potatoes, and peanuts, crops that the boll weevil had no effect upon. In 1919, when the peanut crop yielded more than a million bushels annually, the monument in the form of a fountain, was erected in Enterprise.

The inscription reads:

> *In profound appreciation of the Boll Weevil and what it has done as herald of prosperity. This monument was erected by the citizens of Enterprise, Coffee County, Alabama.*

Strange—how we come to be grateful for something that once seemed devastating!

But what the town fathers should never overlook is the human response to the ravaging of the cotton crop. The really important thing was finding the proper stance for dealing with the problem.

Many people yield to self-pitying despair when something happens to them that turns life's smoothness rough. There are others whose faces become masks of bitterness, and whose voices take on hard, rasping tones.

But there are those who have disciplined themselves to regard every problem as a challenge to be met and used as a spur to drive them forward into new ventures. These are the ones who later erect monuments to honor the difficulties which they used to serve them.

I know a man who nearly a quarter of a century ago was brought low by an illness which threatened to spell the end of everything for him. It looked like curtains.

But with the help of an understanding doctor and the sustaining love of his wife, he regained his health— actually achieved a measure of health and happiness that he had never known before his illness.

This man tells me that he would like to build a monument where he could see it regularly in passing, a monument with this inscription on it:

> *In deep appreciation of an illness that in the Spring of the year 1953 visited me, and for the priceless values it obliged me to seek and find in myself and in others. Thanks be to God who helps us turn misfortune into good fortune.*

17. Don't Say Impossible!

"Nothing will be impossible to you."
—Matthew 17:20c

Before you pronounce any situation of your life impossible you might consider this—you can jump the Mississippi!

Most people think of the Father of Waters running its wide lazy course through the American Midwest down to New Orleans impossible to leap over.

This is the way we react to a lot of things during the course of a week. We declare them to be impossible. Can't be done. Not only are they impossible but it's just plain stupid even to think about them.

So that just about finishes it, wouldn't you say? But before you refuse to take a million dollars—if somebody offers it to you—for jumping the Mississippi, ask some questions like "How wide is it at its narrowest point?"

Now you're thinking.

I've mentioned this to two people recently—both from Minnesota. They smiled and said yes, they'd do it for a million, or a thousand, or maybe even five hundred! Not only would they jump it, they wouldn't even get a wet foot doing it.

Is there something these people from Minnesota know that easterners don't know? Yes, there is. It's the fact that in Minnesota, at a town called Cohasset, where the Mississippi begins its vast, meandering course, anyone can step across the narrow trickle without any trouble at all!

Every person owes it to himself to take a close look

at the half-dozen or so things that he regards as impossible, to see if they really are.

There may be some point at which you can exert a minimum of physical and mental energy and actually do the thing you thought you could never do.

Right now, take a look at your "impossible" list. You have one—everybody has. Take that catalogue of impossible things and look at it honestly, intelligently.

There's a fellow human being who lives on the far side of a vast canyon that separates you from him. Nothing that you could do, say, or think could ever bridge that vast chasm. It's an impossibility—and it's sheer folly to expend energy on the impossible.

But just a minute . . . What have you ever done besides think how impossible it is? If you would honestly explore the situation, you might find a point in that unbridgeable gulf where you could toss over a word, a glance, or gesture, that would lay down the first slender filament of a bridge between you.

Study the other items on the list, and challenge their right to the august, forbidding status of "impossible." Reality is frequently more friendly and cooperative than some of our notions about it.

18. Find the Right Handle

"I cannot go with these; for I am not used to them."
—I Samuel 17:39

"Everything has two handles—one by which it may be borne; another by which it cannot."

These words from the wisdom of the ancient Greek Epictetus reveal possibilities in situations which may otherwise seem impossible.

We all know one or two persons who always seem to pick up their responsibilities by the wrong handle; consequently, they present a picture of pathetic defeat. They seem worn, defeated, pessimistic. Life is just too much for them, and they let the whole world know it with every grunt, sigh, and grimace.

On the other hand, there are those wonderful people who seem to find the right handle for everything and so live their daily lives with grace, gratitude, and hope.

To accept difficult situations as a challenge to one's inner resources is one way to handle some of the really troublesome problems of human life.

One of the worst possible ways to handle adverse circumstances is a self-pitying attitude—looking at the situation with a jaundiced eye and saying, "Why should this happen to me!"

A sense of humor is an excellent handle for dealing with some of the negative aspects of life. Every serious circumstance has its funny side, and it is helpful if you can find it.

Some of the truly wonderful people I know are those who deliberately look for the funny side of their own personal problems.

One of the really positive ways to accept negative

circumstances is to view them as opportunities to join yourself more closely to the whole human race.

To accept illness, going gray, growing old—and all that this last entails—as your share in the common life of the human race is beyond doubt one of the most creative ways of handling some of the conditions to which our human flesh is heir.

Our troubles often unite us, whereas good fortune may alienate us from large segments of mankind.

Persons who pick up their human ills and misfortunes by this handle discover that they can not only bear them more gracefully, but they deepen the channels of their relationships with their fellow human beings.

For those who believe there is an Ultimate Meaning attached to human life, the best way to deal with circumstances that cannot be changed is to use them as a means of drawing nearer to God.

Among the brightest, most radiant souls of earth are those who have learned to capitalize upon their human ills to deepen their relationship with the Ultimate Meaning which abides in darkness and in light.

> Nearer, my God to Thee, nearer to Thee;
> E'en though it be a cross that raiseth me.

19. Extend Your Life's Boundaries

"That which is born of the flesh is flesh, and that which is born of the Spirit is spirit." —John 3:6

Have you ever heard of the woman named Edith who, it was said, was bounded on the north, south, east, and west by Edith!

This can happen to a human being who habitually contracts the boundaries of each golden day of life until his own skin, hair, and nails form the day's outer boundaries.

How far out lie the limits of your days? How vast, how narrow are your horizons? Like the quiet waters of a millpond, life will make way for ever-increasing circles as a stone is tossed in, or for the miniature circles that quickly fade as a tiny seed or a wood splinter drops onto the still surface.

Children are thrilled at the spectacle of the expanding circles reaching out to the farthest shore. So, they select larger and larger stones—partly for the splash and partly for the circles. They revel in the expansiveness of the ripples spreading across the surface of the water like a gracious smile on a human face.

By and large, the happy people are those men and women who keep pushing out the borders of their day-by-day existence, refusing to let their own skin become equivalent to the frontiers of reality.

The unhappy, miserable, complaining people are the ones who confine the experience of a day to the north, south, east, and west extremities of their own physical being.

A woman wakes up in the morning with a headache,

and says, "Oh-h-h, so it's going to be that kind of day . . ."

And that's the kind of day it becomes—because she lets her physical feelings make it so.

Somewhere close by there's a lovely flower growing. Somewhere there's a glorious view of the sunrise. Somewhere there's another human who aches for the companionship she could give—if she would only extend the periphery of her world to embrace more than herself.

Robert Louis Stevenson wrote many of his most interesting stories while sick in bed suffering alternately from chills and fever.

If he had let his own physical feelings determine the frontiers of his existence, *Treasure Island* would never have been written.

Beethoven wrote some of his greatest music after he lost his hearing.

Sidney Lanier, the great American poet, was dying from tuberculosis when he sat on the edge of the vast marshes of Glynn County, Georgia, and wrote—

> As the marsh-hen secretly builds on the watery sod;
> Behold, I will build me a nest on the greatness of God.

20. Keep Your Life Adjusted

Time to love . . . —Ecclesiastes 3:8

Tucked away among my earliest memories is one of my watchmaker father bringing a watch to proper adjustment. After reassembling what seemed like a myriad of minute parts, he would synchronize the watch with the large master clock on the wall, whose ponderous pendulum swung back and forth with irreproachable regularity.

It was not sufficient, I recall, for the watch to be in adjustment while suspended from one of the dozens of hooks in the green felt-lined observation case, its normal upright position. If it proved reliable in that position, it was laid on its back and brought into adjustment horizontally.

"It has to run right in all positions before I let it go," I've heard my father say.

Then he turned it upside down and tested it, and next he tried it at an angle. He wouldn't return it to its owner until it was adjusted for all possible positions that it might be placed in, including riding in a man's pocket or on a woman's wrist.

Life is so much like this. A person has no sooner brought himself into some kind of adjustment with a particular situation, place, or age than he has to adjust all over again.

So, a well-adjusted person has to keep on adjusting himself if he is to stay in harmony with a changing world. Today you're thirty-five with two young sons, let's say. Soon you're forty-five with sons or daughters who stand at eye level or above you. Then you're sixty-five and your children have children of their own, and you—well you're a grandparent!

So it's adjust and readjust as the hours tick away. It helps considerably in keeping adjusted if you have some master device to check your life against—like that big old clock hanging on the wall of my father's shop.

For some people who have managed to keep their lives adjusted through many scores of changing years, there's a master principle they trust implicitly.

In their twenties, they began to grasp the meaning of love, and gradually it became the greatest thing in their lives. In the midst of the changing values and tumultuous events of those years, it was love that gave their lives meaning.

Then as they swung into their thirties and the responsibilities of family life became a dominant concern, it was that same growing love that managed that happy chaos and brought it to order.

In the fifties, if not before, the grandchildren came, and the same concern was felt again. There was a new role, but the same love.

And with the coming of grandchildren came the passing of their own parents, and the sense of loss and loneliness. Then, too, it was love that kept them going, and returned the smile to the face and the lilt to the voice.

The secret of an adjusted life is the realization that, whatever the day, the hour, the circumstances, it is always time to love.

21. How to Rout the Hounds of Fear

Resist the devil and he will flee from you.
—James 4:7

Fears are barking dogs that turn tail and walk away when you stop and look them straight in the eye.

Occasionally I ride a bike—for exercise as well as the sheer fun of it. But my fun was frequently diminished by the fun that dogs derived from trying to scare the daylights out of me as I peddled down a country road.

From suburban ranch houses and urban cottages the dogs would emerge at the spectacle of the lone bike rider, and chase after me, snapping at the turning wheels and trouser legs.

At first I thought I could outride them; but they kept up with me, barking and snapping more fiercely the faster I moved.

The dog threat was about to discourage me from cycling through the open country when I hit upon the idea of confronting the canines one by one as they attacked, and demanding their retreat.

It worked! Beagles, terriers, poodles, spaniels—one by one I met them, stopping the bike, looking them in their eyes, and commanding them to withdraw. Each of them, confronted by the bike rider dismounted in the road glaring at them, turned with a few suppressed growls and headed back toward its own territory.

Only once did I have misgivings about the effectiveness of this kind of confrontation. The dog was a big Chesapeake Bay retriever. Out of the corner of my eye I saw the massive chestnut form streaking toward me.

I was his target; there could be no doubt. His bark was a low, steady growl. He was gaining on me. I could almost feel the jaws closing on my right leg, the side he was coming from.

Frankly, I was scared. Should I risk confrontation with this canine that was certainly a cut above anything that I had confronted up to now—in size at least, and also in the concentrated intensity of his attack? There was nothing else to do—unless I wanted to peddle the rest of the way in shreds.

Jamming on the brakes suddenly, I leaped from the bike and glared at the onrushing retriever. With this, the dog stopped in its tracks. Afraid to take my eyes off him, I outstared the beast. Finally, with a few stifled growls he turned and headed home, looking back over his left shoulder occasionally to see if I had weakened.

Fear of failure, fear of illness, fear of loss of vision, hearing, and mobility—these are part of the pack of barking dogs that haunts the mind of every man and woman.

Whatever you do, don't try to ignore them or outdistance them. Face them, and they'll turn away and leave you alone.

22. How to "Case" Your Fears

"You will know the truth, and the truth will make you free." —John 8:32

There was a noise in the middle of the night. Still darkness was invaded by a sound. One member of the family, awakened along with the rest, whispered that it sounded like a head of cabbage dropped from the roof of the cabin. Another said it was like the impact of a human body fallen from considerable height.

Lying in bed, half awake, half asleep, it was easy to let the imagination paint various and sundry horrible pictures in the mind.

Perhaps a night prowler had stumbled over the redwood table and was now hiding quietly out there in the darkness beneath the great oak tree.

A noise in the dead of night is quite a different class of noise from one that occurs in broad daylight. It has a way of surrounding itself with all the fears of childhood plus the anxieties of the later years—like a magnet drawing iron filings.

What to do about it? Try to fall off to sleep again as though the whole family hadn't been awakened by the strange thud directly outside the louvered windows? Impossible.

So, out of bed. Quietly. Reach for the flashlight. Step carefully out into the long hallway. Open the cabin door. Tread softly along the earthen path among the trees. Follow the beam of the flashlight.

Suddenly, there it was, directly in front, caught in the shaft of light. A branch had taken this hour in the middle of a quiet summer night to sever its connection with the tree of which it had been a part for at least twenty-five years. Why this hour of the night for leave-taking?

All that was necessary was to reach down, pick up the branch, and drop it to the earth, testing the sound produced. There was a thud like that of a cabbage dropped from the roof, or a human body fallen from considerable height.

"Sound like that?"

"That's it," came the reply from within the cabin.

Many men and women live with thoughts and fears that can easily be "cased" in this way. Their minds are like darkened movie theaters on whose screens are projected ghosts and goblins, specters and spooks, and a thousand other frightening shapes.

The mind does not have to be plagued this way. If a person has courage to stir himself, to get up and take a close look and listen at every frightening creak and groan and flickering shadow, he will burst into laughter when he learns that the awful sound of a body falling is a tree branch, and the creak in the stairs is not an intruder stealthily ascending them, but the natural expansion and contraction of wood subjected to changing temperatures.

Jesus said, "You will know the truth, and the truth will make you free."

23. Stuck in a Corner?

"The place is too narrow for me; make room for me to dwell in." —Isaiah 49:20b

One of the daily tragedies of human life is that in a world of infinitely expanding possibilities for new and refreshing experience, many people let themselves be pushed into a stale little corner of existence.

One of the understandable reasons for this is the fact that most of us want to keep life simple, manageable, and safe. If we can establish some workable pattern of action and reaction in the midst of life's complexities, this is precisely what we will do.

So, we run a familiar little groove across the surface of life and stay in it. Whatever we can handle from our groove we handle. Whatever experience would oblige us to get out of our groove, we never experience.

Hence, there are people living in New York City and its environs who give the appearance of knowing their way around the town. They board and exit from subway cars and busses with an ease that astounds the visitor, who is obliged to ask questions and consult his map in order to locate the places he wants to go.

The plain fact is that these New Yorkers seem so expert in getting around in the city because everyday they're travelling in the same familiar little groove between home and their place of employment.

Some of them will confess they have never taken the ferry out to the Statue of Liberty. They've seen the great monument only on postcards. The Museum of Modern Art with its spiral ramp and art displays is as unknown to them as Siberia.

They have succeeded in simplifying life for themselves in a large city; but they've permitted their familiar little pattern to push them into a corner where the atmosphere has become stale and the daily groove-running has become almost unbearably boring.

The cozy pattern of their lives is not merely a convenience; it offers a considerable measure of security which they might otherwise lack.

Primitive people were no more superstitious in sticking to their taboos than many modern people are in sticking to their behavior grooves.

There's something safe about the familiar and always something menacing about the strange—even though the two are separated by only a few city blocks. After all, who knows what might happen if a person should go home another way?

If all you want is to avoid the challenges of new experience, for convenience' sake or for safety, you may well end up in a corner where you see the same people, deal with the same ideas, and hear the same tired opinions expressed day after day.

But if you want to live your life, then risk some new experiences! Get out of your rut, your groove, your weary little corner—and live!

24. How to Make Life Less Boring

"From this time forth I make you hear new things, hidden things which you have not known."
—Isaiah 48:6b

Life doesn't have to be a boring business, but admittedly it is for many people—young as well as old. Why is it? How can it be made otherwise?

"Boring" means "getting deeper and deeper into something at just one point." This is the way we drill holes. It's also the way we create lives of boredom for ourselves and those who are close to us.

There's enough variety among the elements of everyday life to keep us from ever becoming bored—if we make use of them.

On a piano there are fifty-two keys. With these keys all the loveliness of music is created. The variety is endless, and the satisfaction, measureless. But take one of those keys and plunk on it for an hour. You'll feel like screaming.

Take a few of the elements of life with which all of us deal everyday, and consider the infinite variety of possible combinations they can produce. Think about time . . . place . . . perspective . . . persons . . . effort. What makes life boring is keeping these elements always in the same relationship to each other.

It has been said that a person who travels by the 8:15 A.M. train after using the 8:00 A.M., can find a new world. Just that one change in timing can bring him in touch with people and circumstances he didn't know existed.

Take any street corner of a city or town. If you pass that corner at the same time every day, you see the same flow of traffic, the same slant of the sunlight hitting shop windows, the same people. Pass the corner an hour later, and many things will be different.

For an experiment, get up some morning and feel the rare freshness and innocence of those early hours before man and his machines and machinations take command of things. The morning doesn't have to be clear; let it be cloudy, foggy, frosty—there's something fresh and new awaiting you out there.

On a recent foggy morning, when a heavy gray curtain hung in the air, enveloping houses, trees, and rural mailboxes, I saw on a half-dozen trees, spider webs that had trapped tiny beads of morning dew and with them festooned the naked tree branches.

Holding a magnifying glass close to one, I was thrilled at the sight of delicate droplets clinging to a frail filament draped between two branches of a pine tree. At the gossamer thread's upper terminus the droplets were so minute that only the magnifying glass could reveal them. Descending the loop they graduated in size. On the upsweep, they diminished again. When I excitedly announced what I had seen to my wife, she joined me in rapt wonder.

Life doesn't have to be boring—we make it that way.

25. Don't Let a Problem Blot Out the World

"Take the log out of your . . . eye, and then will you see clearly." —Luke 6:42

"Look, daddy, my finger's bigger than that whole building!"

The building, a gray massive structure, loomed a block down the street. And the finger—well it was a little boy's finger, slightly thicker than a pencil—was being held up before a wide blue eye.

I suppose we all remember those days when we were becoming acquainted with the principle of perspective (without knowing the English language well enough to call it that) when a finger held up before an eye would blot out a whole city block, to say nothing of insignificant items like busses and people.

What the little boy did with his finger, many adults are inclined to do with a problem. There it is, rather an insignificant problem (financial, physical, domestic, or personal); but if we make the child's mistake of holding it too close to our source of vision, it will appear bigger than everything else put together.

Outside, children are playing. Men are working in their gardens. Down the block a new house is under construction, and if you listen, you will hear the happy sound of a hammer driving home a nail, and a saw ripping through a piece of lumber.

Clouds float lazily through the sky above the housetops, daring the church steeple to stick them. Nearby a woman sits close to her window reading a letter from her son. In a driveway a teen-ager is

61

working on his cycle. Holding your problem too close blots all that out.

"But the problem is real!" you insist. "It's not something I'm imagining, for pity's sake!"

Of course it's real; there's no denying it. But just because it's real, you don't have to hold it up in front of you all the time until you can't see anything else.

Try putting it out there with those other things for a while—out there with the world of people and flowers and trees and sunsets. Then you'll see it as a part of life, but certainly not all of it. That way you can handle the problem; but you can't and you won't if you give it an advantage over sky and sea and mountains and God by holding it constantly before you.

Naturally, there will always be something nearest you; that's inevitable. But be careful what you assign to that position nearest you, because whatever it is, it will determine how or even whether you'll see all the rest.

Instead of holding your problem closest to your eyes, or your mind, let it be your faith in the greatness and goodness of God that you hold there. This will not blot out anything, since it is not opaque. It's a transparent lens which brings all things into focus.

26. Loneliness—Causes and Cures

"I sat alone." —Jeremiah 15:17

Of all of the experiences known to mankind, loneliness is one of the most difficult to manage.

Picture Robinson Crusoe after the shipwreck, gazing vacantly at the sea that had swallowed ship and crew and all else that had been part of his familiar world.

Many a person who has never been stranded on a desert island has experienced this same kind of loneliness. So universal is the experience that everyone has known it at some time.

Loneliness is longing—for old familiar faces and places. One cure for this is an intelligent, dedicated cultivation of the present.

"Oneliness" is the feeling that you are the only one who has ever felt, thought, or suffered as you do. So it helps to realize that you are part of the human race that knows or has known experiences that match your own.

Naysaying—saying no! to life by refusing the sights, sounds, and persons around you—is another factor underlying loneliness. The cure for it is to develop an affirmative attitude toward your present life and circumstances. Go slowly—but go affirmatively.

Emptiness is the Old-Mother-Hubbard's-cupboard feeling. The cure for this is hospitality to new ideas, experiences, and acquaintances, in order to take up some of the empty space inside you.

Lovelessness contributes to loneliness. No person who knows how to express love will long be lonely. Begin today to learn to love!

Indifference—not caring—leads to loneliness. People who "couldn't care less" about what is happening around them are asking for deepening loneliness.

Narcissism: this term taken from Narcissus, the youthful mythical character who fell in love with his own reflection, describes many people who see only themselves in any situation. This makes for loneliness.

Envy of another person's health, friends, possessions, or happiness is another thread in the fabric of loneliness. A person can help himself by making a sincere effort to "rejoice with them that do rejoice."

Seriousness breeds loneliness. Life calls for a dash of seriousness, of course, like cantaloupe calls for a dash of salt to bring out its flavor. But many people are more serious than is good for them. Life has its funny aspects, and we need to cultivate the habit of seeing them.

Silence intensifies loneliness. Every human being needs to hear his own voice speaking forth from the depths of his personal experience.

If you're lonely, you do not have to stay that way. Identify the causes of your loneliness, and then do something about them.

27. Shatter Lonely Silence with a Song

About midnight Paul and Silas were ... singing hymns. —Acts 16:25

For people who are feeling blue, here's a suggestion—sing!

It goes without saying that when you're feeling low you don't feel like singing. But that's just when you need to sing.

It's good to sing when your heart is merry; but it does you more good when your heart is heavy.

There's probably no activity that more quickly and effectively lifts low spirits. There's no better way to begin a day—even before your first cup of coffee! Remember, you don't have to feel like doing it—just do it, then see how you feel.

I'm not sure I understand all that's involved; but I know something happens when a person breaks the silence barrier with a heartwarming old hymn. The heavy gray smog begins to lift almost instantaneously, and he feels lighter, freer, happier.

Low feelings feed on silence. As long as you just sit and think about a situation that depresses you, you're very likely to become more and more depressed.

The secret of the enduring popularity of "St. Louis Blues" and other blues songs, together with some of the great spirituals, may well be that they offer words and a tune for a person when he's down—so that he can get up again.

So, if you're feeling low, don't keep it all to yourself. That way you risk getting lower and lower. Start singing—not because you feel like it, but because you don't.

Singing when you're feeling low is an act of defiance. As people mature, they may forget the exhilaration of spirit that comes with the daring lift of the chin, the flexing of the muscles, the rebel shout. There are not many "becoming" ways to express this in the years past sixty, but this is one of them and should not be overlooked. Singing in the face of adversity is the soul's defiance. It is shouting into the threatening darkness, the encompassing gloom, "You will not defeat me!"

Another redeeming effect of singing through your low moods until the skies lift is that it takes you out of the loneliness which invariably comes with low feelings and unites you with the tens of thousands of other souls who through the years have sung their way out of the dark.

Best of all, your "song in the night" will lift your soul into the presence of God. You can believe in God in silence; but in the singing of a hymn, you experience the Eternal Presence.

When you penetrate the silence of your depressed solitude with words like "A mighty fortress is our God," you feel you're marching with throngs of fellow human beings down the avenues of the ages. You're not alone. You're not depressed. You're singing!

28. Moving Toward Love

Jesus . . . for the joy that was set before him endured the cross. —Hebrews 12:2

One of life's necessities is the feeling that you are moving toward something desirable, each step you take carrying you nearer, each experience serving to bring it closer.

Convinced that you are moving toward something you truly desire, you can endure and perhaps even relish hardships which would otherwise discourage and frustrate you.

Have you ever seen the picture of the lowland farmer making homeward tracks in the soft mud of the rutted road with his wooden shoes, his hoe and rake balanced on one shoulder?

The picture suggests that the day has been arduous; the long trek home, wearying. Tired muscles, muddy lane, the drag of wooden shoes add up to a difficult last mile.

But in the distance, at the edge of a dark line of trees, stands a little cottage—home. So what if the day has been hard, the way rough? The farmer is nearing the place of fond experiences. Awaiting him is the warm tenderness of his wife, the happy faces of his children.

When a person feels his life moving toward something that has value to him, it matters not how rough the road, how hot the sun, how heavy the burden.

It is only when life seems to be moving away from all that gives it meaning that it becomes too difficult. When every step moves one away from what is desirable, then life becomes an experience of quiet desperation, silent misery.

Is there something we can always be moving toward, some goal which glows upon the horizon of every day? Is there something toward which life can forever tend?

Yes. Even in a world where we are obliged to move away from so many things which have meant life to us, there are still values toward which each day's journey can move us.

The greatest of these values is love. There is no experience known to mankind that cannot serve as the road to a deepening love.

A woman I know lost her little son through death. She felt that life could not go on. But after her grief was spent, she experienced a deeper love coming to birth through her soul's travail. The face of the little boy grew radiant in her mind. Then other faces surrounded it, the faces of many little boys and girls, a cluster of bright, innocent cameos.

Walking over the paths of her large estate in the rolling hills of northwestern Delaware, the woman began to visualize buildings where there were none, school buildings for boys and girls she had never met.

Finally a school came into being, and with it came those fresh young faces she had seen in her mind. Running and playing through the lights and shadows of the large estate, hundreds of children came, responding to the love of the mother who had lost a son.

29. When You Feel Like an Ant, Act Like One

"The Lord is my rock, and my fortress . . . in whom I take refuge." —II Samuel 22:2-3

"I feel like an ant in the path of a stream roller," a man confessed to me recently. He was expressing the feeling of defeat which sometimes moves in upon the mind.

For an ant confronted by these circumstances, there are several alternatives. It could convince itself that "things aren't really as bad as they seem," that the grinding noise getting closer and closer is not a steam roller at all.

Or it might accept the grim and dreadful fact and say in resignation, "All I can do is hope it won't roll over me!"

A third alternative open to the ant is to face the total situation realistically: "It is a steam roller coming . . . and I am an ant . . . and I am right in its path."

This is complete realism. A partial realism would accept only the fact of the steam roller and its ant-ward course. Complete realism accepts that fact, plus the uniqueness of being an ant in a world where there are steam rollers.

With the magnitude of the danger accepted, and with its own true ant nature recognized, the ant is now prepared to deal with its situation.

Steam rollers are big; ants are small. But in an ant's world, everything is big. If the steam roller crunching toward it is huge, so are the pieces of gravel among which it is crawling. As a matter of fact, they are like mighty rocks in a dangerous land.

So, following a pattern of total realism, the ant crawls down from the peak of a mountainous piece of gravel and slips in between it and another piece a half-inch away.

Now the roller is coming closer, grinding, crushing. Now it's going over! The gravel mountains tremble, gripped in cosmic convulsion. Looking up from the valley between the two projecting gravel mountains, the ant is aware of the heavy steel roller passing directly overhead like a gray cloud moving over the mountain tops.

With the steam roller past, the ant crawls out from between the pieces of gravel which have been pushed closer together by an eighth of an inch and makes its way safely among a thousand other valleys between other towering peaks.

The moral of this bit of *ant*hropology is that there is more to reality than threatening circumstances; there are also vast resources to help us face it.

Don't underestimate your human nature. It is the product of tens of thousands of years of human encounters with fires, earthquakes, wars, pestilence. Since, as Job observed, "man is born to trouble as the sparks fly upward," he is also accustomed to trouble and to conceiving ways to deal with it.

In addition to the strength of human resource, count faith in God. If trouble is big and you are small, hide yourself in the shadow of that mighty Rock until the calamity is passed.

30. Life Does Not Have to Be Drab

"Stop and consider the wondrous works of God."
—Job 37:14

> For, don't you mark? we're made so that we love
> First when we see them painted, things we
>   have passed
> Perhaps a hundred times nor cared to see.

This is Fra Lippo Lippi speaking in Browning's poem of the same name, talking about the sheer wonder of ordinary things which we appreciate only when someone has "caught" them for us and spread them out in bright colors on pale canvas.

"Things we have passed perhaps a hundred times nor cared to see..."

Like wind moving through a field of wheat or barley on a clear summer day;
Ripples playing on the surface of a quiet pond or lake or the V-shaped wake of a wild duck paddling its way through the water beyond the lily pads and cattails;
The sun dropping down behind the trees like a great orange balloon at the close of a hot summer day;
Dew hanging like beads on morning grass, droplets of red, orange, emerald, purple changing from one color to another with the varying light;
Shadows frolicking down a sidewalk beneath a row of maple trees;
Green moss clumped at the foot of an oak, looking ever so much like an aerial view of a jungle as you bend close to the surface roots of the oak tree;
The bright eyes of a little child, wide with expectancy and delight;

The lacy reflection of trees in a lake, making one wonder where earth and sky and water begin and end;

A gull's flight above the foaming whiteness of a breaking wave;

The intricate, restful wonder of an ancient root or fragment of driftwood;

The millions of tiny frost mirrors on a dry leaf, exploding into light as the morning sun strikes them.

These were what Browning was thinking of as he spoke through the lips of the medieval artist Fra Lippo Lippi.

We live in a world of ineffable beauty—of lovely scenes we pass a hundred times and therefore label commonplace. We really see them only when an artist or a photographer with an eye for their loveliness captures them for us.

The eye of the artist is not a gift presented to one and denied the rest. We all have something of it left from our childhood—before the bright colors became sooted over by too much concern for other things. "The cares of this world," Jesus called them, which rob life of its freshness and keep us from the kingdom of God.

This paradise can still be ours, and bright hues can come flowing back into lives made dull through living too many hours removed from the glad, sensate world of our childhood. It can still be ours—if we have the maturity to become as little children in the presence of life's wonders and mysteries.

31. Use Your Five Senses

That which . . . we have seen with our eyes, which we have . . . touched with our hands . . . —I John 1:1

Few people ever experience a wholehearted confrontation with life. Their contacts are fragmentary—fleeting brushes with reality.

Ask any friend or acquaintance to describe some familiar object in terms of how it looks, feels, sounds, tastes, smells.

Try him out on an ordinary lead pencil. Will he tell you it is smoothe to the touch, like a crystal from a chandelier; that when you sharpen it, you detect the distinct scent of cedar?

A person could be forgiven for not being able to report this kind of detail about a pencil, but what about for the characteristics of a close friend—the sound of his voice, the color of his eyes, the way he smiles or frowns.

The unfortunate fact is that many modern people just do not use their five senses in their encounters with life. So, their impressions at best are incomplete, vague, and fragmentary.

After living sixty or seventy years, they may have only the vaguest impressions of many significant features of their own life. The whole thing is like an album of blurred photographs representing schooldays, courtship, marriage, children, work, and vacations.

One reason the memory of older persons performs better in the recall of earlier rather than later experience is that in that early freshness they lived more with their senses. At some point along the way they took leave of their senses, you might say, and dealt with experience more in terms of ideas, concepts, principles, and the like.

Even one's personal faith must be based upon vivid sensual experience. Faith does not bypass the senses; it travels them as far as they will go. Then it continues in the course they were following when they reached their limits.

Beyond doubt, one of the loveliest expressions of personal faith is the Twenty-third Psalm, in which a shepherd poet describes his faith in God in terms that only one who had related himself to life through his five senses could have used: "green pastures" . . . "still waters" . . . "rod and staff" . . . a "cup" that "runneth over."

Here is faith taking over from a fully tasted experience. Anyone reading this psalm can almost smell the lush pastureland where sheep are munching, see the reflection of a quiet sky in peaceful waters, feel the strength of a staff cut from a strong tree, sense the cool flow of an overrunning cup.

For a better memory of present experience, for a more satisfying relationship to the world of nature and human nature, for a more deeply meaningful faith, enter into life through all of the senses God has given you; and if one or more of these senses should fail, use the remaining ones more intensely.

32. Plant a Garden

And . . . God planted a garden. —Genesis 2:8

It was early morning. Faint fingers of sunlight were reaching down through the early morning fog. When we tucked ourselves in the night before in the comfortable cabin beds, we heard the perky call of the whippoorwill skipping through the night air. Now the bobwhite had taken over for the day shift, its sharp two-syllable call sounding the reveille of a new day.

Beside the road that runs by the garden I met her, our country neighbor, her gingham sunbonnet pulled down on her head, her past-seventy frame clad in the carefree attire of a woman accustomed to rural ways, who has work to do and wants to be ready for it.

"Morning, Miss Bertha," I said.

Smiling happily she replied, "Mornin'."

"How's the garden?" I asked.

"Come see," she said, with a swish of her apron. Beside an apple tree, whose blossoms were lying in a round white pool beneath it, we looked out over a dozen rows of growing things.

"See my onions," she pointed gleefully.

I saw them, their thin green rattail tops pressing up through the dry sandy soil.

"Over here's my peas . . ."

I looked, and there they were, fresh and green in the amber light of the sun as it wedged its way through the early mists.

"Wonderful, isn't it?" I said.

"Oh, it is, it is!" she said, and there was a little excited bounce to her body as she talked.

"You're young at heart, Miss Bertha," I told her.

"Maybe too young at heart for my age," she smiled coyly, beneath the expansive sunbonnet.

"No—never," I protested.

Later in the day I saw her walking among her chickens, working out by the woodpile, always with the same glad, carefree manner that marked her as a woman who knew herself, her age, her world and wouldn't have any of it any other way.

What was the secret of her joy? I didn't ask her; but I surmised that much of it had to do with that garden beside the county road, almost hidden among the large trees. Digging in the earth, planning, planting, nurturing the little growing things during spring and summer days—then planning what to sow the next spring, thumbing through seed catalogues and inspecting the seeds saved from the good watermelons and cantaloupes that were so luscious on last summer's dining room table when she invited friends in to share them with her.

There's no better advice for a person who has been too long indoors with old, nagging thoughts than "Plant a garden." If you can't plant a garden, plant a window box. If you can't do that, plant something in a clay flower pot, something that you can water, feed, and watch grow.

33. To Know One Good Old Man

"The good man . . . brings forth good."
—Matthew 12:35

I think that to have known one good old man—one man who, through the changes and rubs of a long life, has carried his heart in his hand, like a palm branch, waving all discords into peace—helps our faith in God, in ourselves, and in each other, more than many sermons.

These words from *Prue and I* by George William Curtis hint that the edifice of our noblest faith may rest less upon foundations of stained glass and organ music and pulpit oratory than upon values which pulse with the rhythm of the human heart.

This certainly does not mean that man can take the place of God, rather, that God somehow seems nearer in the presence of a good man.

If you would examine the foundations of your own personal faith, you would discover that far from its being made up of impersonal, philosophical, and theological elements, it is more like a photograph album of many fond, familiar faces, or a choir of blessedly familiar voices.

Wherever they may be, and whatever circumstances may attend their lives, men and women will never surrender faith in God as long as there are human beings here and there who while pursuing a human existence, embody the values of the good, the true, and the beautiful in their lives.

Those who disclaim any serious belief in a transcendent goodness may declare that their conclusion is based upon some academic or scholarly process of logic, but in their hearts they know that the real reason for their negative faith is the fact that in all their experience there has never been what Curtis calls "one good old man."

One might wish that the word "old" were deleted from this lovely quote; but if it were, it would lose much of its force. In the sense of its use here, it means—as always it should mean—a life lived long enough to have tested the values which some of us in our younger years hold only tentatively and provisionally. Do some of the bright colors wash out with use? Is love a real thing in the battering and buffeting of many years? Ask the person who has lived with them through the sharp winds of many winters, the heat of many summers. Ask the old!

If any person on some bright Sunday afternoon, when he's more inclined to give thought to such matters than perhaps at other times, should decide that he wants to do something for the world, he might well consider the desirability of growing old with the truly lovely values of life—faith, hope, gratitude, praise, and love—and let his life be a proving ground whereon these values are tested for emerging generations. Then when people see him and sense his presence among them they will be obliged to resort to better than dollars-and-cents values in accounting for him and for what they feel in themselves as they spend an hour or a moment in his presence.

34. One Good Old Man

We are afflicted . . . but not crushed; perplexed, but not driven to despair; . . . struck down, but not destroyed. —II Corinthians 4:8, 9

I saw him after the spring storm, brooding over his tulip bed like the spirit of God brooding over the face of the deep.

For hours the heavens had thundered and flashed. Hail like grapeshot fired from an enemy cannon had been loosed upon the tender greening earth in merciless volleys.

And now the aging man was out on the battlefield, bending gently over the frail, broken flowers, as one by one he placed the crimson-crowned forms side by side in the basket hooked over his arm. He was chaplain, medical crew, and burial team.

For weeks he had watched the first stirrings beneath the blanket of pine needles in the triangular bed of earth in front of the manor house where he lived in the ninth decade of his years.

Then, when the air seemed warm enough, with a three-pronged rake he gently removed the pine covering, and the delicate green spears reached upward toward the blue of quiet skies.

Day by day he watched them as spring sunlight and occasional showers gently coaxed them up inch by inch, until they stood tall and beautiful, their lovely heads nodding in the breeze as though affirming life's goodness.

"They're beautiful!" I told him, standing beside him on one of those afternoons as he tidied up the bed for his lovely flower children. "How long will they last?"

"Couple of weeks, I guess," he said, his eyes smiling at me through the thick cataract lenses. Thoughtfully he contemplated the joy of so long a life for his precious red tulips.

Then came the storm, and the unmistakable thumping of hailstones on the roof and against window panes; and the old man's heart grew faint within him.

What could I say to him now, out there, his basket filling with the lovely broken forms of his tulip children?

Dare I tell him what I was thinking?—that to me there seemed a strange contradiction in nature if from the same skies could descend life and death?

No, he knew all that. He had faced and pondered the apparent contradiction a hundred times, more or less, in his near one hundred years of life.

Life had not always dealt with him gently. His years had been swept by many storms. Love bestowed had not always been returned. The gentle voice had not always been met with gentleness. The kindly deed was not always received with kindness.

But through it all, he smiled. He would not give up believing because all did not believe; nor would he smite the smiter or curse the lips that cursed him.

Life is richer for me and for many others who have been privileged to know this one good old man.

35. Your Life's Prevailing Winds

A great and strong wind rent the mountains, . . . and after the wind . . . a still small voice.
—I Kings 19:11b, 12

Somewhere I've read of a forest where the trees bend toward the east, this in spite of the fact that when storms howl through that region, the trees of the forest bend like the bristles of a brush in the opposite direction.

Observing the beleaguered trees bowed almost prostrate toward the west during one of the area's worst storms, a stranger to those parts noticed that after the storm had subsided, each tree, as though beckoned by some invisible finger, straightened, then bowed itself once more toward the east, as before the storm.

"It's not the storms, but the prevailing winds that make the difference," said a native philosophically.

In human life it is the constant influence which shapes us also, either leaving us at peace with ourselves, or filling our nights and days with torment.

It is not the ups and downs, but the plateaus that count. What is your living plateau? What is the abiding posture of your soul? After the storms have swept through you and abated, and the unusually joyous times that come and go have come and gone, what is the continuing "meantime" of your life?

It will depend upon the prevailing winds which blow through you. If when the storms die down and you've cleaned up the wreckage there's a steady, if ever so gentle wind of faith or hope or love whispering through the branches of your soul, all will be well with you.

I know a woman whose life has felt the fury of the

gale, the tempest, the whirlwind. Standing on the sandy soil of her farmland that reaches from a pine fringed hollow on the east, to a thicket of small oaks on the west, she recalled the storms of her life.

There was the time of the big fire, when she wakened in the night to see the sky red over the barn. She roused her husband, and they stood a moment, framed in the bedroom window, shocked as they realized what was happening.

"Lost the whole thing," she said. "Barn, stock, everything."

Then came the awful day when her husband fell to the earth while plowing, mortally stricken with a heart attack.

"Then there was the war," she recalled, "and one day we got that letter from the government about Robert being missing in action."

The experiences had rocked her to the depths of her soul; but now, as the summer day was ending in a quiet sunset over her land, she seemed almost serene.

Let the storms rage—as they have and will again. You can't stop them. But when the thunder has delivered its last rumbling blast on the horizon, and the heavy clouds disperse, and the sun is bright again in blue skies, your soul will be what the gentle, prevailing winds of your life have made it.

36. Your Invincible Surmise

He was in the world, . . . yet the world knew him not. . . . His own people received him not. . . . We have beheld his glory. —John 1:10-14

"Sometime, somewhere, in a radiant, all-knowing moment, all that I am as a soul will stand revealed."

Have you ever thought this—felt it in the depths of your being?

Though it may tarry, it will surely come—some moment of total recognition, acceptance, and appreciation of what you are, of what you are worth—the unspeakable, priceless essence of you.

It is a perennial dream—or is it a dream? It outlasts the passing of childhood's and youth's dreams. It survives the disappointments and disenchantments of the passing years. You might call it every person's invincible surmise.

It survives days and years of plodding anonymity, unrecognized capacities, unpraised effort. It is the bright hope sustaining the life of the soul through all of the lusterless hours.

Morning after morning, the woman rose, went to the kitchen, prepared her family's breakfast, ironed their clothes, packed lunches, tidied up the house. In the newspaper that came to the door she read of the great achievements of others. Their names were bannered in headlines. She did not envy them. She loved her work, her family, and that was enough.

But in her heart she sometimes wondered. She had been a pianist and might have made a career of music. But she fell in love with her husband, a good but poor man, and so in her forties found herself in the kitchen for the seven thousandth time, doing the same things, unheralded, unsung. No flourishes, no fanfares, no trumpets—just the same kitchen sounds, heard thousands of times before.

Cyrus Dallin, sculptor of the statue of Paul Revere that stands majestically against the background of Boston's Old North Church, lived fifty-six years after completing the statue before it was accepted and erected.

Competing with well-known sculptors like Daniel Chester French, who sculpted *The Minute Man,* Dallin was only twenty-two at the time, an unknown from the West.

In spite of this, he won the commission, but the judges were criticized for assigning it to one so little known, and the whole project collapsed.

Without the recognition he deserved, the young artist continued his work. Today his *Appeal to the Great Spirit* stands before the Boston Museum of Fine Arts.

In October, 1940, fifty-six years after the rejection of his statue, Dallin saw his *Paul Revere* at last accepted.

Every person must make his own appeal to the Great Spirit in the years of his waiting, knowing sometime, somewhere, he will stand revealed at last.

37. Recapturing Life's Lost Chord

"Oh that I were as in the months of old, as in the days . . . when his lamp shone upon my head."
—Job 29:2-3

In every human life there's at least one peak, a summit upon which one has stood and viewed life in its most sublime perspective, felt the grandest meaning of existence, breathed the rapturous air of personal fulfillment. Thereafter, life becomes a series of efforts, conscious or unconscious, to regain the beatific heights.

I know a man who spent his boyhood in the West Virginia hills in the home of his grandparents. In the old farmhouse, surrounded by other grandchildren, many of whom were his age, he felt ignored and unwanted.

Nothing he said or did won any significant attention. Nothing, that is, until near the end of one long hot summer, when the yearling calves that had been born during the pasturing season were being brought in from the range back in the purple hills.

One by one the yearlings were led in from the highlands until the barnyard was teeming with new life. But one was missing. They knew that old Bess, the Guernsey, had given birth in early spring; but her calf was not with her when they found her and led her back to the barnyard.

There followed days of futile search for the yearling. Then when it appeared that the family had given up the search, the little boy set out alone, threading his way barefoot through the valleys, along the mountain rims, beside the banks of gurgling mountain streams.

Finally the boy sighted the yearling grazing all alone in a stand of lush grass in a shaded valley. Moving slowly so as not to frighten the animal, he threw a slendar arm around the yearling's neck, caressing its soft damp muzzle.

He had gone off without a rope, so his arm had to serve the purpose. Exultant, the boy set out toward the farmhouse leading his precious find.

When the young animal balked and halted in its tracks, the boy tugged on the lithe young neck until he had it moving again. He was aware that his feet were bruised and bleeding where the sharp hooves had trampled them in the contest.

"It was the greatest experience of my life," reflected the man recalling this boyhood rapture. "My grandmother made me a special supper that evening, and the other kids were told to leave me alone—that I had done something that nobody else had been able to do."

This was the answer to the question why the man had made himself sick in his middle years, working harder than anybody else, attempting the impossible, trying the unheard of. He was unknowingly trying to recapture that lofty peak of his boyhood days, seeking his lost chord.

What he needed to know, and in fact came to know, is that the marvelous feeling of being respected and cherished can come to him again and again and remain within his soul as an abiding reality—if he accepts on faith the love of God.

38. A Certain Grace

Set your hope fully upon the grace that is coming to you. —I Peter 1:13

What was this feeling that came drifting into her mind at the close of a hectic day? Everything that could happen in a twenty-four-hour span had happened, it seemed.

In the morning the heater was off and the house was cold; so, there was a hurried call to the repair service. Later in the morning a call came and a woman's voice announced that there had been some trouble with the truck, and it might be evening before the servicemen could get to the house.

So the woman bundled up, put heavy stockings on, and opened all the drapes to let the sunlight in to help warm up the house.

When she turned the stove on to fry a few pieces of bacon, it refused to work. So, another call. They were sorry, they said, but they were "tied up" and couldn't get there until tomorrow afternoon at the earliest. So, she settled for cornflakes that morning.

She went out to the mailbox and found a letter informing her that an old friend of many years had died several days before.

So went the day. But with the coming of evening there was this other thing, as different from the day's difficulties as though it were from another world. The day was discord; it was harmony. The day was strife; it was peace.

There's a certain grace in life which softens the coarse husk of experience and breathes into fate's dank cave a warm breath of reassurance.

It isn't something that can be programmed into life's clicking schedule so that you can say, "Now it will come!" It has its own times and seasons, its own laws and reasons. Call it unpredictable, erratic, or irregular, it is still one of the blessed surprises of our human life.

Like morning sunlight reaching through the chinks in life's dull house to lay down bright shafts across a time-littered floor, it simply comes.

A bright angel moving in some darkening plain or through gathering dusk, it enters into our experience. It is not part of the grit and grime of life, though it is not a stranger to them.

Rather it belongs to a higher order, a realm where what should be is what is, where wistful wish and reverent prayer find their answer in reality.

Once you have felt the touch of grace upon your life, you will never forget it. A thousand bitter days will never blot from your mind the warm recollection of its visitations.

In your darkest hour you will somehow expect it, though you would never presume to command it or to predict the hour and minute of its coming.

But when the darkness is deepest, and hope closes its eyes, it will come; and with its coming all will be well with you.

PART THREE
The Souls of All Seasons

39. The Beautiful People

Abounding in thanksgiving . . . —Colossians 2:6

If I had the choice of the kind of people I would like to spend the rest of my life with—whether on a desert island, in a small town, or in the city—I would say, "Let them be grateful people!"

Physically handsome they need not be, chronological youth they need not possess, wealth they need not have or ever have had, superior intelligence they need not display. But God, may they be grateful!

There's a quality about such people which establishes them securely in the highest human estate. They are the truly wonderful people of earth, the beautiful people.

They are appreciative people. They have learned how to say thanks from the depths of appreciative souls. Any slight favor done for them brings that golden response.

They appreciate the wonder of a clear starlit night, a rosy dawn, the smell of fall in the air, an autumn leaf painted with varied hues of red and yellow, a blade of grass, the glory of a puddle that fairly shouts with the mirrored glory of a winter sunset.

They are affirmative people. To them life is good. It is, as Browning put it, "no blot, no blank; it means intensely and it means good." Moreover, they rejoice in the goodness of daily bread, daily breath, daily sight, the daily ration of strength for daily living.

Thankful people are accepting people. They first of all accept themselves as from the hand of God—"for better, for worse; for richer, for poorer; in sickness and in health." In the same blessedly accepting way, they accept and welcome other people into their lives.

To them a bright sunny day is a good day; and so is a gray misty day, and a day filled with the silver of falling rain, and a white-bound day with snow piled high, swirling around the corners of the house and hanging in decorative pendants from tree branches. They are souls of all seasons.

They are humble folk. They think, feel, and live, not from a base of presumed "deservingness," but from the common ground of their share in a humanity that looks to God for every crust of bread that passes its lips.

And they are reverent people. Amid the jungle of tangled horizontal lines that make up everyday living, they have raised a series of perpendicular beams and arched them, so that they live in a temple where their voices are heard in the morning, at high noon, and through the vesper hours, singing "Holy, holy, holy . . ."

40. The Best Thing You Have

They gave according to their means ... and beyond their means, ... but first they gave themselves.
—II Corinthians 8:3-5

"Whenever I talk with him I come away with the feeling that while we were talking he slipped a thousand dollars in my hand, winked, and said, 'This is for you, enjoy it!'"

The youthful dark eyes were alive with pleasant memories as the young man sought words to describe one of the most vital relationships of his life.

It is this way in genuine friendships. Rich treasures pass from life to life in the hours that are shared together.

Our enthusiasms, joys, interests, humor, faith—these are the priceless traffic between persons joined together in genuine friendship.

How many years does a person have to live before he realizes that the most precious thing he possesses is himself—his own soul? All other values pale beside it. And when he shares this deepest, truest part of himself with others, he is bestowing upon them gifts far surpassing the value of diamonds.

What could enhance the value of the priceless? All other things have value only because they are related in some way to the eternal value of the soul.

What would be the value of a diamond in the mines of Kimberley, South Africa, if there were no admiring human eye to behold it, no human soul to present it to in love?

When will we finally learn that the best we can give another person is not something impersonal, whatever

93

price tag it bears, but something as close to the soul as the soul itself?

Many of the unhappiest people in the world are those who have been given everything except the deep, sincere love that comes from another heart.

The greatest giver may be the one who inwardly says, "I have no silver and gold, but I give you what I have" and then gives himself.

An older man who had nothing to give to a younger friend involved in a financial crisis gave him three hours of his life one afternoon—listened to him, talked with him, encouraged him. From that afternoon on, the young man's circumstances improved because his attitude toward himself, toward life, and his fellow man improved. That made all the difference.

The years beyond sixty are years when a person shares whatever he has come to possess with grandchildren, children, neighbors, friends.

In the blessed season of your giving, don't overlook the best that you have to give. Find a way to share yourself with others so that in time to come they will feel that you have left them something priceless.

41. Be a Good Listener

There is a friend . . . closer than a brother.
—Proverbs 18:24b

Few persons who read the novels of Nathaniel Hawthorne have ever heard of Sophie Peabody, but until Hawthorne met this frail invalid, he was an unproductive recluse of a man, who could only brood over his stifled and frustrated creative urge. Sophie Peabody became the dynamic sounding board into whose ears Hawthorne poured out his plots, descriptions, and dialogue.

"Do you understand what you have done for me?" Hawthorne once asked her, when his ability as a writer began to win public recognition. "You have revealed me to myself."

This heartfelt confession moved Sophie Peabody to speak her own feelings. What she told Hawthorne was that through his loving interest in her every thought and word, she was beginning to recover from the illness that had been with her since childhood.

Beyond doubt, one of the greatest things that any person can do for another is to listen to him, listen with all of the doors and windows of his soul thrown open in the other person's direction.

Many a person is a stranger to himself until some friend sits down and gives him a chance to speak from his deeper levels of thought and feeling—to tell what he thinks, fears, hopes.

Actually, Sophie Peabody did not reveal Hawthorne to himself, as he put it; he revealed himself to her, and thus caught glimpses of himself in her eyes. As he talked and heard his own words—his voice quavering at times with emotion, at times calm and reassuring—he gradually realized who he was and what were the heights and depths of his own hitherto unexplored mind.

Any person who has a friend who will hear him through when he feels his soul must burst if he keeps silent a moment longer should thank God for one of life's most precious gifts.

My own dearest friend is my wife. With her I talk out all of the fears, frustrations, hopes, and dreams of my life. And she listens, with all of the doors and windows of her soul open toward me. To her I can confess the worst that is in me, as well as the best; and she listens to both.

She is the testing ground of my ideas and plans. No more would I drive to New York, board a plane, and take off for Europe unannounced than I would launch any serious project or publish a single line without discussing it with her.

Any human being who really wants to be a friend of man in this world will cultivate the simple, gracious art of listening.

Through this as much as any other single thing a person might do for another, life is strengthened and individuals grow in their appreciation of each other.

42. Priming the Old Pump

"Give, and it will be given to you." —Luke 6:38

There's something quaintly reassuring about an old pitcher-head pump mounted atop a length of pipe rising up out of the dry earth.

The first rusty squeak is unpromising. The iron handle hangs loose in the hand. But just pick up that cup of water left on the rickety old pump bench for the single purpose of coaxing the pump to reach down into the depths and fetch up the clear cool treasure of silent subterranean streams, and pour it down the top of the pump . . . Easy . . . Not too much too soon . . . Now work the handle, and you'll hear the old pump begin to groan and gasp asthmatically. Then you'll feel the handle stiffen, telling you water is on its way up through the wire mesh filter of the pump point twenty or thirty feet below the surface where it was driven years ago.

Then it's there, right before your eyes, clear and cool as it was for thirsty Abraham in that weary ancient land of his sojourning.

"You've got to give water to get water," the old pump seems to say with an occasional groan as you continue to work at the handle. Invest that cup of priming water left on the bench from the last pumping or you'll get no water here.

It's the same with people. To draw goodness up from the mysterious depths of the human heart you sometimes have to pour some of your own goodness into the soul of the other person. Affection, human kindness, understanding, goodwill, friendliness—

you've got to give some of your own to get it flowing in others.

As chaplain, I visited in the wards of a geriatric facility. Many of the patients were responsive to my attention and wanted to talk.

But there was one who lay in her bed like a horizontal Sphinx, expressionless, uncommunicative. For weeks she gave me the silent treatment.

Then one day I stopped to talk with her again and for the first time noticed the cameo she was wearing.

"That's a beautiful cameo," I said. "Tell me about it."

With that the woman became alert. Her eyes met mine, and she smiled warmly. The pin had been her mother's, she explained, and she prized it beyond words. "She was a wonderful woman," she said, "and I'm proud to be her daughter."

For a half-hour or more she talked. I had found the key that opened the door that had been closed to me.

Try this approach sometime. You'll be amazed and blessed by the pure loveliness that wells up from the depths of the human heart.

43. Hate: the Mask of Fear

There is no fear in love. —I John 4:18

Fear has many faces, and one of them is hostility. I've always been afraid of snakes and always hated them; and in the back of my mind I knew there was a direct relationship between the fear and the hate.

A recent encounter with a snake convinced me. Had it not been for a toad hopping through the dry leaves drawing my attention to the spot, I might have missed seeing the snake, stretched full length in the tall grass a few feet in front of me. The snake, aware of me at the same moment I saw him, lay perfectly still.

I must confess my first reaction was fear, and with the fear came the urge to kill. My axe, hoe, and other sharp implements were in the cabin, and the snake lay between them and me.

So, at safe distance I eyed him, and I was sure he had those dark beady eyes focused on me. If I moved threateningly, so would he. As I watched, some of the fear began to leave; and I found myself beginning to see my potential adversary as another creature of God pursuing its own peculiar way of life in a difficult world where snakes meet up with creatures like me whose first impulse is to kill because they're scared.

Then it occurred to me that there was no reason why I should take his life. The world was big enough for the two of us—if I could only get him to move out of my path.

So with the persuasion of a stick gently prodding the sleek tail, I got him going. Obligingly he glided in under the ivy beneath one of my favorite oaks. After he was gone I knew I had conquered some of my fear, and much of my hate.

The vicious, irrational attitudes many people have toward each other are rooted in fear. No doubt they would deny this and argue that they "just plain hate" them and that's all there is to it; but that's not all there is to it.

Somehow it's always more acceptable to us to admit we dislike a person than it is to admit we're afraid of him. If we can settle for disliking him, we can avoid the painful business of self-examination. Why do I dislike him? Well, just because he's not likable. Why am I afraid of him? Now that's a question that brings up a lot of things I don't want brought up.

We're inclined to dislike people if they're different from us. But here again, it's not a matter of dislike as much as it is feeling threatened by the difference. Their color, accent, and manner—because they are different from ours—become a threat to us. The threat produces fear which we can't handle and don't want to admit having, so we transmute it into hostility and act to get them out of our club, out of our community.

If we could honestly face up to our fear of people and see it for what it is, the hostility which is fear's mask would drop off.

44. At Peace with the World

When a man's ways please the Lord, he makes even his enemies to be at peace with him.
—Proverbs 16:7

A deep sense of peace, like Abou Ben Adhem's, comes over a person when one fine morning he becomes aware that his life holds little or no threat to the lives of the living creatures who inhabit with him the same parcel of the good earth.

Take, for example, a recent morning when I tramped over our little island. A frost had fallen during the night and the leaf-strewn ground was like a bowl of sugar-sprinkled corn flakes.

Along the way as I walked, tiny chickadees played in and out of the hedgerow beside me. No one told me, but it was clear that they were deliberately escorting me in my early morning ramble.

Down the road a piece, a rabbit sat as though waiting for me to swing along behind him. As I approached, he hopped ahead a half-dozen hops. The little white powder-puff tail bobbed in the early sunlight. He stopped, turned toward me, and waited again.

After a few minutes of this capering, the rabbit casually slipped into the thicket beside the road and, as I passed the spot, I saluted him with a few clucking sounds that I felt sure he would understand. I knew he was sitting in there watching me.

Farther on, a neighbor's dog slipped silently out into the road beside me without so much as a whimper and muzzled my hand as I stretched it out in greeting.

When a person is at peace with himself, he's at

peace with the world, and somehow the world seems to get the message.

But when a person is in conflict with himself, the world becomes his personal battleground. Any day, any hour, most anybody—man, woman, child—may feel the sharp edge of his unresolved inner conflict.

It is a rule of thumb with me when any individual becomes an abiding source of irritation and difficulty in a business or social relationship to conclude that he's at odds with himself.

The easy-to-meet, easy-to-live-with people are those who have made their peace with themselves. Because they are comfortable with themselves, anybody at peace with himself can be comfortable around them.

They are the genuinely good neighbors, good friends, good husbands, good wives, and good parents. To be near them is like drawing up beside a friendly fire on a cold night.

45. Keep Your Lights Burning

"Let your light . . . shine." —Matthew 5:16

When the new family moved into the old farmhouse perched precariously on a Vermont mountainside, they were unaware of the effect of their arrival upon anyone except themselves.

One day the husband and wife met a little old lady who informed them that she lived in the small house in the valley, pointing it out with a gesture of a brown, weathered hand.

"Be you the windows across the valley?" she asked warmly. The man nodded tentatively; then catching the lady's meaning, he said, "Why, yes . . . yes, we live up there."

With this the little lady told them of the comfort and cheer it gave her to look across the valley at night and see their windows lighted up.

"Be you going to stay and keep your lights burning, or maybe be you not?" she asked.

That evening the man and woman returned home and took down all the shades and curtains from the windows which faced the valley.

Stepping outside into the dark of the Vermont night, the husband and wife strolled down the mountain a short distance. Then turning they looked up toward their new home. The curtainless windows filled with light were like beacons sending their shafts down into the little valley.

Then they turned and gazed toward the small cottage swathed in darkness, a faint oil lamp glowing through one of its windows. Smiling warmly into the night, the couple turned and climbed back up the slope.

"What was that she asked us?" the man said thoughtfully, taking another long look down into the valley. "Be you going to stay and keep your lights burning?"

The old Vermont house high on the slope embraced the man and woman with new warmth as they slipped through the massive door and closed it behind them. They knew that down in the valley there was a little lady who was grateful for their light.

Whatever light you have, let it shine. More than you know there are eyes waiting for it and hearts hoping that you will stay and keep your lights burning.

Do you believe that in the human heart there is a capacity for love and that when everything else fails to make a difference, love can? If you believe that, you are the keeper of a light. Let it shine.

Do you believe in God as the divine meaning behind human experience, the eternal support beneath the structure of life? If you do, don't keep your curtains drawn. Open them, and let that light of yours out into the darkened valley. Down there in the night, lonely souls will see your light and thank God.

46. The Hurt and the Healing of People

Every one helps ... and says ... "Take courage!"
—Isaiah 41:6

People need people; there's no denying it. Even the hermit soul who lives out his existence in physical isolation from the rest of the race needs to know that the rest of us do exist out there beyond his lonely hills.

Without the human race his withdrawal would be without meaning. His solitude would have no significance without the multitude from which he has retired, and about whom he thinks night and day, if only to remind himself that he is no longer one of them.

Our worst hurts come from people, but so do our greatest joys, our most stimulating challenges, our noblest inspirations, and our happiest self-realizations.

Most everyone at some time has set himself against the human race, thanking God that he is "not as other men are"—unreliable, deceitful, hypocritical, mercenary.

But after all is said and done, after we have licked in loneliness the wounds we have received from others and glared defiantly at the whole human race from some imaginary height, it has been a warm word from a fellow human being or a kindling glance or handclasp that has set things right again.

Oh, we hurt each other all right; there's no doubt about that. But in the providence of God who declared, "It is not good that man should be alone," we also help to heal each other.

It is in the most intimate relationships that we receive our deepest wounds. No one can hurt us like a dear friend or family member. When the question was asked, "What are these wounds in thy side?" the reply was, "These are they that I received in the house of a friend."

Most of us have quoted at some time that cynical comment, "God protect me from my friends; I can take care of my enemies."

Only in close relationships do we let down our defenses and render ourselves vulnerable. Because someone who knows me better than others do knows more about my weaknesses as well as my strengths, he or she can hurt me more than others can.

But it is also in the close relationships that healing comes. Only one to whom I have entrusted my innermost thoughts and feelings can understand me, accept me, love me—and so heal me when I am wounded.

So, let's get into the business of living with people. Talk with them; listen to them; laugh with them; weep with them.

You'll get hurt, but you will also find healing, not on some far away hill in exile from your brothers, but with them.

PART FOUR
The Ultimate Relationship

47. A Higher Point of View

"My thoughts are not your thoughts, neither are your ways my ways. . . . For as the heavens are higher than the earth, so are my ways higher than your ways and my thoughts than your thoughts." —Isaiah 55:8-9

One of the roots of the despair and deep soul-weariness which afflict many modern people is the notion that the way we see things is the only way to see them, the way we think about them is the only way to think.

On an autumn vacation, I climbed Stony Man Mountain, one of the peaks in the Appalachian chain south of Washington, D.C.

Standing on the rocky brow of Stony Man I could see miles up and down the Shenandoah Valley. Through my binoculars I was able to distinguish remote farm houses, see fences bordering harvest fields, and even follow a farm truck barely visible to the naked eye as it lumbered along a deserted valley road.

From where I was perched, with an autumn breeze fanning my face, I could see the little cabin I had left an hour or so before. At this altitude, its cozy relationship to the other cabins, nestled snugly amid great oaks and hemlocks, was apparent.

If your view of life has become jaundiced of late, it might be well to keep in mind that it is not the only view of life. Weary thoughts mulled over a thousand times are not the only thoughts there are.

More than we might realize, we view life through the clouded, distorted, lenses of hundreds of ideas, concepts, prejudices, and fears which instead of bringing us closer in touch with reality, alienate us from it.

When we were children, we were told what a tree was, and so we continue to see all trees through the lens of a single, pathetically inadequate idea. Along with trees, we learned about cows and horses and people—the whole creation, heaven and earth.

Then, along the way, other ideas were added—some scientific, some financial, some economic, political, or psychological. This was our "education," and we hoped that it would help us to interact intelligently with reality. But rather than help us in making sense of what we see and experience, this accretion of facts on our lenses dims and distorts our vision.

What we need to consider is that there is a mind aware of all that we are aware of and more—much more—but in a clearer, less frightened, less despairing way.

Historically men have called this awareness God. But it makes little difference what you call it so long as you are aware of it and you somehow sense that your very existence is more intimately related to it than to any other fact or relationship of your life.

48. Without Majority Vote

"Who has known the mind of the Lord, or who has been his counselor?" —Romans 11:34

Few experiences are more impressive than a thunderstorm in the night. Moving in on a cool breeze that whistles softly through the screens, it builds up to a gale that sends paper flying from desks and tables.

Then comes the lightning thrusting its mighty lances through the darkening sky. Distant thunder rumbles like breakers on faraway beaches.

Soon the rain is barraging rooftops. Windows and doors slam shut. Hurried steps are heard in the streets as late walkers take refuge.

The lightning grows sharper, returning the colors of day to nearby houses and shrubbery. Thunderclaps that sound like the splitting of mountains fill the darkened intervals.

Now the rain is washing against closed windows, sluicing down rainspouts. The blacktop road gleams in the lightning flashes like a polished boot.

Gathered in homes beneath the pelting rain, families move closer together, as if by some primitive instinct subtly transmitted through the long generations of man.

Quieted by the cosmic spectacle, children ask earnest questions of their elders as the TV show, unwatched, goes on.

Such experiences will always serve to remind human beings of their kinship with the elements, of their utter dependence upon phenomena that are as independent of the human mind and will as if the two never existed.

Every man awakes each morning in a world where

the sun rises without his assistance, as Henry David Thoreau, the philosopher of old Concord, once reminded himself and others.

It is sobering, and humbling, to realize that emerald waves would crash against the craggy arms of Maine's shoreline if there weren't even a solitary lobster fisherman to witness the scene from his boat.

And the full moon would rise into the night sky at the proper time of the month if there were no terrestrial keepers of the calendar.

Rain would fall from the heavens, and snow, and hail, if the United States Congress never met again in Washington or any other place.

This doesn't mean that we human beings aren't important. We are—but in a secondary kind of way. The point is, all our seeing, feeling, hoping, dreaming rely upon an amazingly trustworthy system of natural laws and elements which came into being (and are maintained up to this moment) without one word, one thought, one single act on our part.

There is an Intelligence, above man's, in whose hands all things in heaven and earth exist. When your all-too-human life becomes confused, and you feel defeated and undone, pause a moment. "Be still, and know."